THE LITTLE BOOK OF GUESSES

Also by John Gallaher

Gentlemen in Turbans, Ladies in Cauls
(2001)

For Eric / Well Met And Good luck On Your Journey — Good Speed

THE LITTLE BOOK OF GUESSES

POEMS / JOHN GALLAHER

❧

Four Way Books
New York City

Distributed by
University Press of New England
Hanover and London

Editorial Office
Four Way Books
POB 535, Village Station
New York, NY 10014
www.fourwaybooks.com

Library of Congress Catalogue Card Number: 2006928239

ISBN: 978-1-884800-77-1

Cover art: Cedar 17 by Louise Belcourt. Private collection, courtesy of
Jeff Bailey Gallery, New York.

Cover design: K. C. Witherell/Hello Studio.

This book is manufactured in the United States of America and printed on
acid-free paper.

Four Way Books is a not-for-profit literary press. We are grateful for the
assistance we receive from individual donors, public arts agencies,
and private foundations.

Distributed by University Press of New England
One Court Street, Lebanon, NH 03766

Funding for the Levis Prize was provided in part by a generous donation in
memory of John J. Wilson.

[clmp]
We are a proud member of the Council of Literary Magazines and Presses.

ACKNOWLEDGMENTS

The Alembic: "Measure Twice, Cut Once"
The Black Warrior Review: "Cursing the Darkness *&* What's it to You"
The Boston Review: "A Guidebook to the Afterlife"
    "A Guidebook to When Things Were Better"
Colorado Review: "The War President's Afternoon Tea"
    "How to Haunt the Living"
Court Green: "Concerning Our Stunt Doubles"
Crazyhorse: "Pockets of Resistance"
    "General Conversation *&* the Like"
    "Anecdote of the Field"
    "Daily in the Birds of the Sky"
    "Lost in Our Creations, We No Longer Believe in Falling"
FIELD: Contemporary Poetry and Poetics: "Hot House Hottentots"
    "Campfire Girls at Sunrise Hill"
    "My Life in Alcohol"
Hotel Amerika: "Thicker"
Indiana Review: "*&* the Quonset Hut as Well"
    "Ephemerana"
    "Opportunities for Seeing Things"
The Iowa Review: "A Guidebook to Everybody's Business"
The Journal: "All These Effortless Afternoons"
    "Our Recent Stay in Thataway"
    "The Other Confession"
jubilat: "In the Book of Nothing"
Lake Effect: "Pretty, Popular, *&* without Secrets"
LIT: "You *&* Your Lover Embodying Silence"
    "In the Book of the Disappearing Book"
The Ohio Review: "A Guidebook to Some Foreign Country"
PLEIADES: "The Cloud from the Machine"
    "Cocktails at Six, *&* It's Like We Won"
    "Landscape with Suicides"
Ploughshares: "Only Lovers *&* Believers, Please"
Quarter After Eight: "The Perspective of Disappearance"
The Southern Review: "Ghost Children"
    "In the Little Book of Guesses"
Verse: "Sunshine for No Regrets *&* No Residue"
West Branch: "A Moment in the Market of Moments"
    "No Encores. No Autographs."

"When I Say *World* I Mean *Please*" was produced as a broadside for the Underwood reading series, St. Louis, MO.

"A Guidebook to the Afterlife" was set for voice and oboe by Paul Dickinson.

My thanks go, first, to Wayne Dodd, as always, for reading this manuscript in several versions, for your guidance, for your generosity, and for your friendship. I am grateful to all those who have been there during the writing of this manuscript, for your conversation and for your support. I am thankful, as well, to the RustList, for the time away. April 2006, ROTM.

Many thanks to all at Four Way Books, with special thanks to Martha Rhodes for her example and her acumen, and to Kathleen Ossip and Sally Ball for their keen and sympathetic reading. Finally, I extend my gratitude to Henri Cole for selecting this manuscript for publication.

CONTENTS

III

IV

*What would life be like
if the second world war
had actually taken place?*

—Ronald Reagan, 1983

choose one:
The Same ☐
Different ☐

Other ____

I

In the Little Book of Guesses

I'll make you up from out
of the living rooms we face,
equal parts singing gate

and people we knew once,
in biographical order. Equal lengths

investiture, and the sun came out
and it was bright in my eyes.

The room is dark behind
the flaring particles. The day
is twenty years ago

and Tuesday. I did not mean
to leave us there with nothing,

as I was saying *car rides*
for *wonderful*. It hardly matters. Unequal parts
wanting to mean something

and frosted glass. Whose cigarette
in the plaid ashtray?

Whose clothes on the coffee table
as the dog begins to bark?

The black dog out in whatever yard,
barking off and on

the rest of our lives.

You & Your Lover Embodying Silence

There's the window. Go ahead,
the sad neighborhood calls and calls.

It hardly matters which room you choose.

The only furniture there, as the words
after those words,
and your clothes all around you—

we will find some use for each other. Help me.

There are too many tomorrows
for tomorrow, for your legs twinning

and falling away. The sky
is pushing always.

Who could stand it?

Pull the blinds from the windows, the windows
from the walls, the walls

from their dark mornings.

In a house with all this space,
you're reaching out.

You're gifting yourself.

LANDSCAPE WITH SUICIDES

Then there was a little bridge that we came to.
Caught halfway through a dissolve.
I would like to be your pocket.
Forge of a hand.
Forge of the locked rooms where the songs are written.
Then the cut of rope. Then the long thin cut.
Back inside, they head for the bedrooms.
Here, where all things are written in the dark rooms, the clock has
    stopped the empty minutes.
So that every picture is chosen by someone.
I would like to be up and down.
Didn't you see the lions singing there?
Didn't you sing once, your hands in the dark, as well?
And the world is ending.
The taken-down world that never was is ending.
We will sing them out of their cabinets and into the woods.
Then the hours the clock has stopped the blank communication.
For the suicides, we will have a little bridge.
Do you remember a little bridge in the dark?
We will have to mention some birds beyond the trees.

Valentino Ponders the Ineffable

I see London. I see France.
Letting my fingers do the walking, counting steps

up the beautiful people.

And it's counting days still, with a big X marking the spot
in both raised and indented relief.

And your legs around my neck.

I see Paris. And skin tastes good
in the sun.
                    And oceans glow. And salt. These

ribbons remain dreamlike
down your wrists. But not me, I'm busy
with this finger and this finger.

It's nice to think I could always get there.

Or that getting
                    is perhaps the wrong question,
as your dampness is right where I left it.

How are such things possible,
and then not? Suddenly not, like a scarf left

on a train, we circle ever wider, ever
further away. I can see that now. To there
and to there, floating in the want
                                        of my body.

And maybe I'm still attractive. Maybe

if I stand over here, away
from the light.

Measure Twice, Cut Once

Afternoon's drone, and first sleeveless day,
the yards are yards again, all at once.
And we're stumbling from our houses. Redbuds waving,
we're stumbling into the light.

If it holds meaning, it's holding it awfully close.
That's one thought. And if this is all,
then there's not much to study for
or tally. That's another, I suppose.

Behind every afternoon
is further mountains. All shimmery.

I'd like to start again. Here, or
somewhere back there, anything
I know I can't have. Where the redbuds started
swaying slightly, seemingly
like some reward.

But they're taking apart this town you just left.
Where you looked so pretty.

The afternoon dances forth—
The afternoon rummages forth—

DAILY IN THE BIRDS OF THE SKY

Desire only leaves you with things.
With things to look at, we moved past the portico.
Several colors: yellow and blue and green, I think.
Which contribute to tone.
On the highway some night, think of us.
It's the start of a new beginning, over the little houses.
Call it your immolation.
Or call it *Terms of the Adoption.*
And each day is like a new day, posting flyers around town.
Discombobulated by belonging here beyond everything.
And when you see a comet, it means that living with a roller coaster
      returns one home constantly.
Which can get no closer than immanent.
Like what they wrote on my birth certificate.
But I'm sorry, I've forgotten your question.
Maybe something music might approach.
To turn to all.
To balance it on one finger, and watch it spin.
A little bubble of unknowing.
A little glimpse of the long afterward.
At the end of thought, where there's only flame.

The Other Confession

Running behind a carelessness.
In the midst of beginning. Is here.
I'm watching my mother crumble by ones.
And maybe it is that easy. Carefully.
And lots of sailboats out there in the old times.
Example of a beginning. A turning loose.
Whose yard is this?
Who lives in that house? That little?
I was standing there watching her as she tried to remember.
Little meaning a great deal is a beginning.
Having a great life.
To whistle the spaces between thoughts.
I was leaning against the kitchen counter.
There was a dinner before her.
Thinking nothing is a beginning there never.
I am not learning what to do.
Remember.
I am looking for the ocean. Have you seen it?
A little spot of blood.
A little spot of blood on the horizon?

Only Lovers & Believers, Please

Clearing by this afternoon, and I know you just want
to have a good time. OK, I'll try

to work with that. Out here in the field, then, with this frontier
we carry around, there's no difficulty.
It can all be explained:

We're here in the scrub with our broken hearts
and the insects, and we're looking for Elvis. Saying
Here's Elvis, or whatever. . . .

Please notify us if you've seen him.

And we're not at all close to completing this thought,
you know, with the bugs and other old tricks.
Rain, even. That we hope for. In the dogwoods.

With only lovers and believers, please.

Understand, we're not under great stress.
And this is only the beginning; the movement could grow.

It's all about capturing the subject's personality and

energy. Over by the dogwoods, as
the sun came out, that might've been Elvis

there. But differently. As we're all
different. Always.

Going around in the great surround.

Statements as Questions

We've been leaning toward people for years, out there
with our inside voices. Surrounded by hyacinth
and purple skies.

I've been meeting their gazes as well, pretty friend.
See it as an act of citizenship, with these neat rows of houses
under fluffy trees, as we're full

of quavery emotions out here. And we've plenty of fluffy trees,
they start from the ground
                        and go all the way up . . .
Call it education.
(Summer night. Blank pages.) And how it's grasped.
This park, say. With lovers

and crickets. A basketball someone forgot, back and forth
slightly in the breeze, as we have our knowledge
and we have our knowing.

I'm desperate to see you, say. Or, *Call me.* . . .

Something is bound to happen
in the understory, among the palliatives.

For the little book of guesses, dark birds
against a dark sky.

I don't know how to comfort you.

On Your Brilliant Escape

In the city of the made-up city,
you can watch them meet.

Desire in the backyard.
Desire down the lane. Wallowing.

You can press
your enormous eye
to their window, and see them
taking it up,

becoming little red birds.

And you can demand they hear you,
there at the light switch,

a fist the size of the opera house.
I'm small. I fall soft,
they could say.

I'm lovely. I know you.

How to Haunt the Living

Picture a child you see walking down
the sidewalk. Across the snow. In the near dark.

Because the future is uncertain, it's winter, quick
as things unwished for.

Let's say you don't know whose child this is,
or it's yours, across the snow. It's winter,

and you haven't lived here for a long time.

You pick up the book you were reading before, and you read a bit,
while distance settles in.

My whole life I will have a fear of something.

Touching the wall. The smoothness. All these years
making a tight circle
                    to some doorbell ringing.

They will think nothing of us, in time.
And these times we fought

for a new chance to straighten it out, easy
as a box-cake, in this warm room, on a winter evening.

And all the missing children are here,
playing with blocks.

Campfire Girls at Sunrise Hill

A very serious undertaking, it is,
the way the interior unflattens
as we press our faces to the garlands

and veils, over these
better surfaces, better maps. So we
motored on down

for the evening.

The trees that were around us were themselves
for a moment. Later, I'm silver
under the stars.

And so was everybody else.
We were no different.

Silver trees over silver girls
on these silver hills.

It was horrible. But that's just
words. I could just as easily
have said wonderful.

Please.

Don't remember me like this,
remember me some other way,

some way I never was.

II

Anecdote of the Field

The children are running across the field, each
carrying something.
Each on his or her spindly legs.
The field's a good field.

And there are wild blackberries to be found, large
red flowers, and birdbaths.
The wind's kicking up behind them.

These children are running to run. They
are pointing
to the grayness of the sky.

Their mouths are all little circles—Oh, they say,
there are so many places to be.

In the next field over, a house
is full of smoke.

It is nice, the children say,
to need to be saved from something
and then to be saved.

It is nice to have bright eyes
and to be running.

Pretty, Popular, & Without Secrets

She walks through the door as the phone rings.
He removes his coat while opening the refrigerator.
They're at home, breathing deep. They're full of air.
It's not an easy time, she whispers.

A little night music, perhaps?
The cessation of weather startled us both,
among the dishes.
Maybe a movie?

What's interesting though, is essentials, as in,
there's this house at the end of the block,
and there's this couple about.
I never knew kitchens could smell so lemony, we say,

for something to say. Back on the sidewalk
they move on north. They walk
down the walk, the one and the other,
a thing among things.

This's a truism, she mutters, as though
thought through, *strictu sensu*:
the look, the easy curve away
into partial concealment, with traffic

all about, wending its way forward. And in this way
we flank the sink, erstwhile (at any rate), these
diners over time, yellow and green
about the edges, with pictures of trees,

where we'll leave them,
now that history's going faster and all,
and our faces are starting to hurt
from all the smiling.

Our Recent Stay in Thataway

It's see no see at the obstacle race, where our thumping feet
or marching feet—our thunderous feet—
go to all sorts of over theres.

So we may be some time at the obstacle race. Where
we tripped or we didn't, with the damn wolves
or dancing wolves

(or maybe some dogs) on holiday. With the obstacles.

Should we just say *just*, maybe? Would that do the trick?
Looking for a lever to pull (part *&* parcel),
or a field of buttercups, off

into the sizeable territory, under compulsion,
with a thin northwest breeze having us loll and weave.

(Can you see a cheerleader out there with a buttercup in her hand?)

We've come a long way, but distance always looked better
from a distance. (Maybe past the tires *&* rope swing?)

Donning our caps and gay apparel, and having
accustomed ourselves to our customized dogs, we've
honed the idea of ideas there in the obstacle race

that'll never catch up. To stake one's reputation on.

Down among the obstacles, with a high-end look and feel,
we've been making chalk outlines
on the decor, whistling tunes.

It's serious business at the obstacle race.
(& our cheerleader & her buttercup . . .)

THICKER

At the bottom of this incline wanders a murmuring rivulet.
The pin oak is wet under a gray sky.
Drizzle softens the edges of the late morning.

I'm noticing something stir in the branches down there.
I'm thinking that yesterday there was a withering desolation in Irene's
    shrunken life.
And sooner, rather than later, I'd like to be seen in aristocratic society,
    but I'm really not much for drinking and mingling.

That's my little dance then, in November's first freeze and lost horizon.
Some branches stirring and low-lying fog, and a telephone ringing from
    someplace close by.

It's entirely different from what last night's report indicated.
Some branches stirring, and maybe some leaves.

I wish I had a bird's eye view of the situation, and could know things.
Examples abound. A car door shutting down the street.
And half my life away.

But the branches down there are much thicker than here around the house.
It probably wouldn't do any good anyway.

Maybe, though, if I'm not moving.
Maybe if I pause, holding my breath, counting.

Sunshine for No Regrets & No Residue

April folding into May, 2005. Four months
into my 40th year, the azalea's finally
started to bloom.

Maybe I could get a career doing this, standing there
at my second floor window, watching one
tree, counting buds.

With original packaging,
and surrounded with household gods,
at my age, I got up this morning.

This is my victory dance
and all the wars: the azalea I planted last spring

is blooming.

The sun's on the dresser, like Audrey Hepburn, young.
Smiling. Like all those kids in Hollywood. There

with something waiting
out in the future,

the sun is on the dresser.

My Life in Alcohol

The things we did, long past the last opportunity to be someone else.
Details in ninety seconds, with big adjectives.
Now we hide everything, after the mistake.
And people are in love anyway.
A little scrambling may be necessary, as was the style then.
And I'm in this poem, there in the 21st row, in the form of disembodied anger.
Asymmetrical, but with balance of form.
So what makes a life anyway, as now it's getting further away.
And within each category, there are many degrees of difficulty, of course.
And the possible margin of error is all week.
Back here, we're busy fearing death, working from notes.
The one labeled "Who Am I."
The one with my brother losing his eyebrow.
And how we're making it through our lived lives anyway, without consolation.
The one where they're thinking about numbers, and making
    announcements over loudspeakers.
One so often doesn't know where one is.
Still to be named, they'll be dredging this river for me in vain.
For I've learned how to float, eyes blank, to the sea.

For Your Married Lover

You will say *previous engagement*, the sunset like travels abroad.
Where they are being two nice people showing their concern.
And each night I'm home.
Each night I'm laying my head against you for a little while.

You will also learn about the days of the week.
I can almost taste it, like earth, in our own Coma Berenices.
Not a day will go by, so many lovers ago, without standing there on the
    other side of the door. 2 a.m.
For your married lover, you will be keeping your own counsel.
Beautiful, like it's always raining.

The light is on over the table, cornfields out the window.
And Libra, the Balance, the Scales, who will be ready to make up a silly
    name, hymn to its own unfolding.

For the things we see every now and then, I will choose only dark countries.
I will wear everything I own.

Let the pickpockets have me.
Let the crows eat my soul.

OPPORTUNITIES FOR SEEING THINGS

It's one damn thing after another. In this
book, for instance, the hero
                              runs off
to a deserted island

with a woman. He's a disenchanted
European. She's a lost soul, covered

in evening. It's one of those exotic places.
And these identifiable subjects
                              momentarily
between reference points. Onward, to the

deserted island, he says, at some point.
Maybe then things will be all right.

And with this romping girl there on a walk in the wilds,
all balmy. And the wilds
                              milling
out in the undergrowth, all these eyes sparking

in the firelight. As scenarios go, I
always loved the postcards there. On the beach,

and in between palms, pale

orange, green and gold, and
white, and rust and brown. Apologies.

My apologies.

& THE QUONSET HUT AS WELL

Out in the back by the high quality metal buildings,
and with an eye to the driveway,
we had something to say about getting older. Our

roofs are round and we're portable, which
helps. With her hair up
in rollers. And terrible cramps.

It seems like there's something I need
to do, but I can't
for the life of me remember what it is.

Maybe let's you and me take
a look at the shrubs. At 8, 7 Central. Guided tours
available daily. And maybe Sadie's your

ugliest friend. As well as those grayer things
in between, like her parents
arriving home unexpectedly. Other

ways in which we eluded ourselves
eluded us for the moment,
cultivating the shrubs for the sake of the shrubs.

You're an ambitious tyke, aren't you? they say
and say. . . . But it was always
a lot of fun out there

in the dark. Technological even.

Pockets of Resistance

One day in Californialand, the Californians
were very busy. It's a rewarding sonic experience,

in the sand
            on the beach, not hiding
anything. And while they're playing, they're
learning important concepts.

They're singing a song. They're walking
on the planks, looking around (observatory
type things). And then

I'm going through the orange groves
in Orange County, connecting the dots. Heading

into the sunset. And the Pacific, one day
deeper, in the several climates there. I
hope everything's just wonderful. I'm sure

it still is, with those field trips
                            off to the field, filling
out the desert.
And four children running, expecting surprises.

It's a near approach to pleasantness,
like a giant coloring book,

out in the brambles and all that,
exploring the color blue. I just wanted to tell you,

I lie awake some nights

thinking, lost
out in those crowds.

You don't have to vocalize every thought you have, you know, Buffy said, down in the mud room just past the drum room. We've a secret, we said. No problem, we said. So maybe hostility keeps us going? And certain kindred ideas. But we've jumped ahead in time. The change was slight. It'll be a souvenir folder of city views, we decided. And that bit about water under the bridge, that was great. So, several friends later, we find the scenery's still good. And how six of us were unfaithful somewhere near the sandy beaches. So what are your goals? we asked her, there in the shower. She decided to write it in a book and add to it from her imagination. The skyline of San Francisco can be seen in the background. She was smiling now. Pasties in space, we say. Then Bruce had sex with Ronald, who was wearing a dress. And the power of the atom, as Bruce told us. They're on vacation, they said. Well, the earth may be round, but the moon's obviously flat. Everything's been proven by a recent study. Just look at it up there, she continues, with her hand in her pants. For many years it was considered the greatest bridge in the world. At least that's what Buffy says. And she should know. And forty-nine moons could fit inside the earth, you know. But she could fit fifty, they say. And she's a penchant for accoutrements and outdoor activities. We've pictures, and excellent intentions. They did a little dance in the kitchen. Their understanding as the work progressed was a blessing. A mass of things. A communion.

Cocktails at Six, & It's Like We Won

We're just pointing out our point of view, they like to say,
but when they started taking off their clothes,
Bob and Carol decided it was time to bug out
of the bridge tournament.

No place like home, is something we say at times like these,
including multiphonics and

resonance trills. Like when my marriages are falling apart.
And the dachshunds were nice this year, too.

So I'm not quite done with redemption then,
or the late, experimental

hors d'oeuvres of George. Don't you just love the olives,
you say, but they look more like words

than things, I'm thinking, over by the cognoscenti.
(Without longing of any kind, by the way.)

Note the examples of logos, George says, off
seeking out the bathroom. It feels like
neighborliness, but the screams from each couple,
although derived from the same basic material, are

presented quite differently. Margo, on the other hand,
was always freely expressive,
pointing to the draperies in ways that are ontological.

It's mostly sunny out there, and seventy-six degrees, in the future, we say.
Ah yes, Margo says, the future. . . .

The future sure was something.

III

In the New Age

In the new age tourism is the answer.
It's cinematic meditation.
In the new age everybody sings over the fields.
We have a very repetitious soundtrack.
We will go to the mountain when it's all the mountain.
We will share one name.
It will be long, in the new age.
How can I mourn its passing when everything passes?
I'm becoming a mystic.
The question of the unmovable question.
The guess of the missing words.
I've already gotten your point, so here's a new point.
The sun is bright and hot in the new age.
The trees blow about.

Happy Birthday to Everyone

Where are my beautiful shutters, then?
On the first day you aren't mourning.
On the road to recovery.
I've always wanted to say *Hollywood Ending*.
And then it turns into people.
And some long roads and wishes, which helps.
It's all part of the process of me being someplace else.
But this is your avalanche, in the future.
With a set of Christmas Yaks and last chance love affairs.
And having many different feelings, even on the same day.
What's it like, living there, then?
And how do you feel about it?
I've been a bad reader.
It's been too many funerals ago.
And maybe it's only a headache, and a cake for a hat.
Where the blowing of the wind is wind blowing.
There is no unity but sequence.
Yes, we say, and we're getting to the chorus, there with the person you
    might love soon.
We're holding out some kind of hope.
It was about lunchtime.
It had several interlocking parts.

In the Book of the Disappearing Book

It's a spring flowered dress that was her effacement.

On a train, and because of what windows do sometimes.
Her face is floating above the landscape
unaware.

I used to think that I was reporting my life to someone.
I was a radio.

I used to think things happening was unfolding.

The trees are blooming all through her
and there's no one to tell.

And the discipline of roads.
The icy discipline of to and from.

In the air of nothing, I used to think
I was understanding distance.

Green God, in your language of silences, tell me.

A Pocket Guide to Some Foreign Country

A long time he considered the book.
When she opened the window, we were surprised
by trees pushing themselves

out of white mist. For years
the years fell in a circle on the carpet, turning blue,
as he considered, in burgundy, in port.

Sure thing Flopsy, we said,
as she opened the windows where several angels
per pin perpend. But that was the old novel.

It'll be arriving shortly to the former room, where
we're looking for ourselves. We're looking for ourselves
and we keep uncovering things, yellow

things, brick things. He considered
the book that coquettes with color, leaning
at the corbel. Would that it were larger, he thinks,

and eminent. Something's just going to happen,
apparently. Someone's coming, the nabobs depend on it,
and their beribboned gewgaws.

Twilight commences where the trees are.
Don't give them the chance to sneak up on you,
we said. Flopsy, we said.

He was indoors and then he was outdoors, with the book.
And we're late, the greens going to turquoise
and the trees adding their gray to gray. If he considers

the book, for a long time he considers himself
considering. If she opens the window, the light of morning comes
to show you things in white.

She was opening the window,
and the cries of linnets that no longer
are the cries of linnets on the hill. She was opening the window,

but that was before the war. A little
snuggery, perhaps, with the clock well into evening,
and the browns, the russets, the deep, dark yellows of that place.

The War President's Afternoon Tea

I was very quiet back then. *Shh*, I'd say.
It's something one does with one's face.

A quiet boy, when everything is pure.
And I haven't changed a bit.

In Texas we call it walking. And now I must live as a child,
picking up blocks. Throwing them.

If the tree causes offense, pluck it out. It says that.
If the map's blank, it's because I am not there.

Up here, we talk about the afterlife often.
Soaking it in. And we're all living, aren't we,

in this fine, white afternoon.
Now watch me make this shot.

Because if you want it to be true
you have to practice.

So I must say what I'm saying.
I must say it over and over.

The bomb went off "prematurely," ripping through a police van. The bomb went off in a popular cafe in Ein al-Helweh. When the bomb went off there was a loud noise. He called May 15 the day the bomb went off. While the first bomb went off at Juwett Memorial Baptist Church at Ongole in Prakasam district of Andhra Pradesh at around 8:30 a.m., the second blast took place while emergency personnel were helping the wounded. It looks like a bomb went off in here. He and his girlfriend Kerry O'Shaughnessy, 28, would have been in the Sari club when the bomb went off. Another bomb went off on a park bench near the US Embassy, injuring nine people. The bomb went off before sunrise, blowing out windows blocks away, shaking neighbors from their sleep. Two bombs were planted in the schoolyard; the first bomb went off at about 9:45 a.m. in a powerful explosion, which blew out some of the windows of the school. And the bomb went off. The first priority was to get as much distance as he possibly could before the bomb went off. A bomb went off in Lhasa on Monday, the sixth reported explosion in the city in the last nine months. He [J. Robert Oppenheimer] and I were lying down right next to each other flat on the desert right outside the control [room] at the time the bomb went off. A fire-fight broke out and one VC was last seen firing into the smoking back seat of his car when the bomb went off. The bomb went off between 10 and 11 in the evening on 24 June, near the City Public Security Bureau (PSB) Building, which is situated about one kilometer north. The bomb went off at the wrong time. I don't think they were inside, but they were about to enter the club when the bomb went off. This car bomb went off outside the South African Air Force HQ in Pretoria. I lived in the YMCA, about 100 meters from where this bomb went off. Tubbs said the warning call made some twenty-three minutes before the bomb went off was a simple, non-specific message. Then on Saturday May 1, another bomb went off at a pub in Makindye and injured five people. There were four days of peace before the bomb went off. Labourer Lakshmi, 26, recalled that she and her 18 month-old daughter Nitya had barely returned from a tea stall close to the eatery when the bomb went off. After the bomb went off, the men sprayed gunfire on fleeing passengers. When the bomb went off we were kneeling in the bottom of it.

THE CLOUD FROM THE MACHINE

The shifting clouds mesmerized Bob, Carol, Margo, and George.
And then we decided to go on in.
That'll set you to dreaming, huh? George said.
But it was really just dumb luck.
Or almost dumb luck.

Remember how we'd look at the sky back then?
Maybe make things out of it?
Birthday cakes, or howitzers.
And our tremendous moral resolve.

And none too soon, I tell ya, George said from the barbeque grill.
And what do you want on your hot dog?

That was when we decided the house would work better as a musical.
Late summer or early fall, 2002.
The details of everyday patio maintenance, maybe.
In G, if you want to play along.

Place has a lot to do with where you are, we decided back there.
With airplanes flying over.

Also startling's the sky tonight, but we've already said that.
Like that dream I had, Bob said, the one where I'm someone else.
The announcer maybe.
We all agreed, as we tend to agree here.
We like ourselves better this way.

Hot House Hottentots

And haven't the flowers been lovely, Jenny wanted to know,
leaning over the lilies, adumbrating one

afternoon, while at the same time effacing
others. Well, it's the environment, we decided.
Still though, it's easy to hum along.

And that's what we were good at back then, 1970-something, with the sweep
of history there behind us. And Jenny standing up

and turning the hose on. Spring, we decided,
and well-watered flora, make a wonderful
combination. Now let's see what else

we can get from the time machine . . . it's
a big blue day with puffy clouds
                              and Jenny's
undeterred and wearing a halter top. A fine coincidence,

the chorus decided, advancing
on the jasmine. Good thing there's lots of distance
there, and vastly diminished versions of bigger things,

we thought. It's not the size of the ship
                              that matters, remember,
as audiences could identify
and began tapping their feet, while the lilies

dragged themselves through the condensation on the glass
and Jenny waved to some

boys from school. Well, more's always an option,
I guess, as we're wiping our brows, there
in the swell days, with what's missing.

But something's always missing.

CURSING THE DARKNESS & WHAT'S IT TO YOU

A lot of trains come through this town all night,
and the kids are experimenting
with expressions again. As in how things are,
or are manifest—and what things do—for the first time
in the history of the world. It's almost comforting.

And we're popping the old antibiotics again.
The clanging of a lot of trains continues for some time,
as Tad and Nancy practice for the rest of their lives.
You look big and strong, says Nancy.
You have expressive eyes, says Tad.

They've great testimonials. They've wonderful,
bright smiles. It's important we remain clear
on this, how sometimes it's just train after train
after train. Cyclical even, as the pipes freeze.
And with the weeds making for the window box,

where somehow it's all gone terribly wrong.
Maybe some crucial details somewhere.
And we wanted each other to have more than that.
So many things, really. While all night
the lights blink, and the cross bars go up and down.

Ephemerana

Back at the beginning again, with those same sidewalks
and tree-lined streets, it was all action.
One action after another all about us, this plucky band

milling with the streetlights and lunch specials.
We're knowing where some things are,
around the things we yearn for.

And then not dying all afternoon.
It's a great example of effective teamwork, like dressing up
and pretending to be someone else.

But when I was in Texas, thinking for a moment
I was in Ohio—Oh look, it's Point A again,
the world falling its way into the world.

Now how'd that happen?
Leaves and trees and flowers and all that.
In orderly retreat.

So then we've found a beginning again,
at the lip of some future
we're hoping to outsmart. And all

these little guesses, where nothing stops.
Where everything just goes
into everything else all afternoon.

Pray for a daughter that's on dialysis and's having three toes amputated. Hocking Hills. The Marketplace. Pray for the cessation of a listener's severe headaches. Pray that a father stops drinking. Happy Hills Park & Camping. Pray for the Good Lord to intervene in a family dispute over property. Dow Lake. Diamond. Pray that a woman'll sell her car. Pray that a husband'll get time off over the fourth of July weekend. The Coffee Cup. Pray for the employment needs of eight listeners. Pray for a listener's marriage and for grace. Green Valley. Pray for a young woman who's anorexic. New Straitsville. New Fairview. Pray that a beloved family pet'll return home. Pray that a daughter'll not get a job in a bar. Enterprise. Pray that severe weather'll miss a good friend's town. General Clay. Pray that a man'll find a job and some transportation. And for a woman to meet her rent payment this week. Riverdale Homes. Discount Center. Pray that a listener'll pass a nursing exam. The Plains. Pray for a listener with many health problems, for her complete recovery. Garden Terrace. Pray that a sister'll leave her abusive husband and for their children. Chauncey. Pray that a father's cancer'll go into remission and for peace in the family. Basket Arrangements & Cut Flowers. Fill Dirt Needed. Haydenville.

IV

In places, Bob and Carol merge into, or become, doors or windows, opening onto a crowded but illegible backyard. As was predictable, a radical change in outlook became apparent in the living room. What a cute baby, we said. We're friendly that way. And what a fine painting, we've one just like it. What's common, besides our basic nonobjective approach, is the extraordinarily large size of our davenports. But life is conflict, Bucky reminds us. These two factors are interrelated, we're certain of it. If only we could remember how. It's the memory that goes first, as dear old mumsey would say. What a great dog, we replied, pulling on the sock puppet. We should take some comfort in that, but we don't. The wall sconce's a new opportunity for working out inner impulses. Well, perhaps, but aren't we jumping the gun a little here? Bucky asked. It's all about pie, in the end. Apple or pumpkin. The rhythms of Peter and Jenny, however, are collusive, changing menus and dinnerware abruptly. I love what you've done with the place, we say. And what a nice old lady. Be careful, it's perishable, Jenny remarks. It's all about lawn care, you know. All in all, most of their days look unfinished and indeterminate. Maybe because there's no conscious process between the original impulse and the application of hours. An amazing cat though, we offered. And it matches the bedspread beautifully. It's all about one's choice of background music, Peter said from the stereo. He's always finding clever places to hide, Jenny said, full of local pride. Not to be outdone, Bucky found references to or reminders of events or feelings in his own life. Well, it's my life's work really, he says, with parts of the guest room affixed here and there. We're sorry, Bucky, we meant to address you more formally, we said. They call each other for as little as 2¢ a minute there, imagine that. We look into space, and space is a long way off. Look closely and you can see them. Looking closer it's all just you looking.

A GUIDEBOOK TO WHEN THINGS WERE BETTER

Now there arose a situation that was to be repeated, off and on, for the next several years. What kind of pills? she asked over dinner. This doesn't exclude the possibility that he sensed his death approaching. I also have my favorite parts. But I never get to do that in my whole life. It's for your own good, they repeat, over and over. That's what they say, but I'm beginning to doubt it. Peter and Jenny finally split along lines partly territorial, partly social and economic. Besides, all their friends were. Frankly, your kids drive me nuts, she said. We came back and she was right (see below, chapter III). Something negative came between Adam and Rosie that night. Rosie couldn't remember inviting Jen. And lately his dreams are about other people's problems. I'd be a great mother if these kids didn't take up so much of my time, she says. I swear I had no idea the damn thing was loaded, he said. It's taken them a week to set up this messy confrontation. We're sorry we missed it though. The kids made a paper swan out of your invitation. Tomorrow, I have to drive out there again and bring them back, diagnosed as they are with malingering, weirdness, and moral turpitude. He's taking treatments now and the prospects look good. Her finger nails are falling out and she says there's this shooting pain up her left cheek, yet nothing specific seems to be wrong with her. We trust you and your doctor are on the best of terms? Peter just can't shake the hiccups. And Jenny's taking those same little green pills. Later it isn't broken after all, but they have to walk very cautiously. A good general rule's to be prepared for anything, so I'm staying here at the clinic. Anyway, you always liked them better than you liked me. I've just been wondering, that's all.

A Moment in the Market of Moments

November is something we were thinking, there
in the traffic jam, finding our

calm centers. (It's my very latest
strategy.) Here in November,

we're feeling scientific.

We're studying reliable sets
of objects. And mostly
                        sets of people

looking straight ahead. At a certain
distance. (Not to mention
ironic asides.) And the clouds

and the traffic going a little into winter,
then not. Everything's
                        rolling up
these days, with

the left lane closed
fifteen hundred feet ahead. And
this long string of brake lights

coming on in a wave,
in the night, in a light rain,

seen as we will. One part.
Another part.
                    The happy world.

CONCERNING OUR STUNT DOUBLES

After plans to meet his birth-mother fall through,
he decides to try his luck with California, on a sunny day.

So what does belonging feel like?

he asks Irene in a taxi on N. Western Avenue,
where she recounts a made-for-TV movie she saw some while back.

And she's not driving all that well either.

Well, who was it then that wrote all that stuff on the back of my
    baby pictures?
Anaheim maybe?
Maybe Santa Cruz?

We thought we'd wait for the movie, we said.
But it wasn't always that way.

Sometimes you just gotta take a chance, as Irene says, fumbling
    with her pills.
Blues, pinks, terracottas: the city's always been bitter this way,
and she's too busy thinking to help us.

We'll not forget that any time soon, pursuing
the mistaken assumption that we'll find what we're looking for.

And the vexed question of the Romantic hero, to boot.

This's the first of many of our chance meetings.
Later it's a movie star and an ex-boxer.

Call it a natural event, like popcorn, there
between the pyramid and the coliseum.

And since I'm adopted and it doesn't matter what my name is,
I'm the creature from the black lagoon. Love me.

ALL THESE EFFORTLESS AFTERNOONS

It's always people just leaving twenty years ago.
It's look at me in my bubble, and the oak door and the oak in the backyard.
No, really, I'm in an office somewhere calling the fishes.
Is this some magical package, I'm asking.
It's principles of pain relief.
It's a phone call can change everything.
The window on the easel is showing green hills and further mountains.
I would've loved to've been there, but my watch stopped.
Which gives us a whole new way to be wrong.
Just look at all the clean beasts in pool, hot tub, or sauna.
They're growing old less gracefully over in the hotel, where we were
    standing there pretending.
I'm riding the trains to stay warm, wearing my conference badge.
They say, sing me something, but we have no such song.
It's where I might end up alone.
They say someone in here breathes audibly.
Tell me the people were standing.
Tell me that people have memories all day.
Where it was twenty years ago, people were just leaving what a turn
    in the road leads to.
As the buildings are tall there, neither side of the street is sunny.
Come, help me up, we're alive, they say.
It's the idea of being someplace.
It's the idea of going.

In the Book of Nothing

In the severance, we have no names.
Maybe they forget to whisper.
Merely, and watching ourselves.
At the funerals of very small coffins, how much pain is there?
And who decides?
She hit her head and fell.
Now we're afterward, in the little book of guesses.
And what I might deserve.
And in what economy.
Snowed up cars float down the street, with our donations and experts.
It's how the lonely find the phone.
It's this tingling sensation when I came across him in his office, weeping.
There at the outline of the door, it's the old story calling to check in.
To see how we're doing.
I'm doing crosswords.
I'm counting by ones.
It's just something the body does, like drowning.
When I was hoping for something else.
Something benign perhaps, like socks, where all we'd say would be
     photographs of spring houses.
This's all wrong, but so many things are wrong.
With this coffin a single man can carry.

General Conversation & the Like

We've been thrown in, we decide, looking up
at the counter girls in yellow
and brown. Midsummer.

A hundred degrees. We honor the moment by silence
and the essential structures
of booth or table. It's a process, I've heard,
with the parking lot steaming.

These are the things we're given to work with
just now, or getting to now,
as we've been awaiting these arrivals

and've been keeping ourselves busy
by referring to things. Glass
and ice rattling. And menus get passed.
Salad or fruit cup.

There's no proper perspective, I guess, but
you can sit over here
for variety. Nice red flowers.

Look at them out in the heat.
They've been thrown in, we decide, looking up
at the clouds
spinning all at once.

Ghost Children

The afternoon's heading for the silences
with my dead dad. Which
is an incidence of travel.

Which is going the length of a short road.

My live dad is beneath the car
with his feet protruding. He's reaching
up behind the transmission.

Because you've got to have goals,
he says. Our lives for them.

And the winter doesn't help a bit.

The ghost children are not patient,
they admit. They've brought

my dead dad. He's
waiting on the counter, thinking
about pool. He's calling

the side pocket. The sun
starts over here

and ends over there, he says,

while the ghost children play with dolls
in the corner. They dance there,
all bursting with sunlight.

No Encores. No Autographs.

When I was little, and could float,
I made up my mind to touch everything
on the way. *Here I go* and

Yes into the red leaves, the winter logic.
Waving seemed so sad
when I was mild, and could hear

the sounds of the house
growing into the hill. The eternal workings
of the going-to-be,

while out to the left
there's a hole in the overcast. A little hole.
It may be growing,

it may be shrinking. Hard to tell.
Either way, it comes back now
without meaning.

It comes back as people I knew once,
fading in and out of buildings and trees
in a north wind,

while, full of spider webs, the porch
glistens in dew and first light.
A foggy translucence covers the world.

You can go out and read the argument
in the grass.
Just take off your shoes.

You can call yourself a pilgrim,
noting the texture of matter.
You can go from here to here.

There Is No Mercy in Heaven

At four, I got a new name that I had to practice in front of the mirror.
New was the prefix of all things at the edge of the world I had to walk upon.
I liked the new yard best of all, full of ice cream trucks.
New road. New mommy calling me in.
I flew in a plane and the pilot gave me silver wings to pin to my shirt.
Clouds brushed me clean, and I was new.
I sparkled, full of forgetting.
Somewhere, I'm up there still, counting on my fingers and my toes.
In the new heaven. Over the new earth.

When I Say *World* I Mean *Please*

We begin somewhat after the beginning, in
the red (pink) shirt, under the blue (white)

sky, I am (or one is) walking (as vectors
by a brook). Breathing in and
                              breathing out with us

this afternoon. Maybe there's something
we could say. I'd like to do some good, perhaps. In a cloud

of commentaries (with news from exotic
                              places)
we're doing all around stuff, in a

park-like setting, generally. (& all the non-arrivals . . .)
Just the wind through the pecan trees.

I was listening to it, over there. And so that it all
becomes more acceptable, I saw
                              someone
who looks just like you. At the trellis. In
the evening. A very nice place.

I thought you might like to know. It appears
someday we'll have a wonderful

future, in the green houses, the red hotels.
No wind at all to speak of.

Everyone accounted for.

Lost in Our Creations, We No Longer Believe in Falling

The starlings are quiet in the look of things.
The trees are not breathing.

There's this place you've got to get to,
where the lovers are not looking up.

There's this thing you'll never know,
though you might listen to both sides of the argument.

And though you meant to stay,
these aren't your people.

Though you practiced your balance, and your special walk,
the rooms are askew.

Voices go by too quickly.
The gestures are intricate, and just past memory.

So let's play the adult game, where you get to start all over again.
Some days, today for instance, you'll close your eyes.

You'll go out and lie in the garden.
You'll begin covering yourself in earth.

John Gallaher is the author of *Gentlemen in Turbans, Ladies in Cauls* (Spuyten Duyvil, 2001) and co-editor of *The Laurel Review*. His poetry has recently been published in *Boston Review, Colorado Review, Crazyhorse, FIELD, jubilat, The Journal,* and *Ploughshares*. He holds graduate degrees from Texas State University and Ohio University and lives in rural Missouri.